Walk with Faith in Jesus

Christian Inspirational Poetry of Faith, Hope, and Life

Marnie Hunziker

ISBN 978-1-64515-894-3 (hardcover)
ISBN 978-1-64515-895-0 (digital)

Christian Faith Publishing, Inc.
832 Park Avenue
Meadville, PA 16335
www.christianfaithpublishing.com

Printed in the United States of America

Contents

Introduction

God has truly blessed me through the years. He has given me many gifts, one of them being my gift of writing poetry. God has helped me through some very tough times in my life. His guidance and words always gave me strength, courage, and faith and has helped me to touch others and share His amazing grace and love to everyone. I am so grateful and thankful for the life He has given me, and every day, He shows me the woman I am because of Him. The day I turned my life over to Jesus Christ as my Lord and Savior was the best decision I ever made. I hope you find these inspirational poems of hope, courage, love, and faith as a reflection to what life with Jesus is all about. He will change your life if you let Him in.

Favorite verses: Romans 8:39 says

> "Neither height nor depth nor anything else in all creation will be able to separate us from the love of God that is in Christ Jesus our Lord."

Ephesians 3:18 says

> "To grasp how wide and long and high and deep is the love of Christ, and to know this love that surpasses knowledge that you may be filled to the measure of all the fullness of God."

I AM Here......

When you feel lost and alone.

Remember I am here holding you in My arms

When you have struggles that are too much to bear.

Remember I am here going through them with you.

When you need to talk and have someone to listen.

Remember I am here listening closely.

When you need guidance and encouragement
    to guide you along your path.

Remember I am here walking right next
    to you every step of the way.

When you feel sorrow and despair.

Remember I am here with open arms to comfort you.

When your heart is broken and it feels like it is in pieces.

Remember I am here to repair and mend it back together again.

When you feel afraid.

Remember I am here to protect you and
    will keep you safe from harm.

When you are going through a storm.

Remember I am here fighting the battle with you.

My child, you are mine and I love you
    unconditionally with all My soul.

Know that I will never give you anything you cannot handle.

You are a part of Me and I will always carry you,
    protect you, guide you, advise you, and comfort
    you all the days of your earthly life.

Until we meet in paradise. Remember I…AM…HERE.

Thank You, God

Thank You for the wind that blows gracefully through the trees,

And for the birds that have their heavenly songs to set free.

Thank You for the peacefulness of every
sunrise that smiles across the land,

And for every sunset as it says goodnight to all is admiring fans.

Thank You for the rain that reminds us of Your sadness,

So we can be all reminded to act in kindness.

Thank You for all the precious children You bring into this world.

What humbleness and compassion they help us to learn.

Thank You for the animals You gave us to touch our hearts.

It is something that each of us will embrace and not let part.

Thank You for the flowers that fill the air with their sweet nectar.

And for the butterflies that paint the sky for all of us to capture.

Thank You for Your holiness that fills our souls each day.

That helps guide us toward Your heavenly way.

There are so many things to be thankful for within this
lifetime. Most of all God, I am thankful for You!

Daybreak

As you smell the dew in the air from the beginning of the day.

To listen to what all the birds have to say.

To watch all the animals scurry around looking for their breakfast.

To smell the fresh morning air you wish could always last.

To see the sunrise all across the sky.

You know in your heart that it was brought from up high.

As we wake up each day, to see what wonderful
things may come your way.

God has given us such beauty from within this world to unfold.

Listen within your heart and see all that He has told.

Remember He is walking beside you and keeping you strong.

For He loves you no matter what might go wrong.

God's Painting in the Sky

*Have you never noticed that there isn't any one
sunset or sunrise that is the same?*

It is like God is painting a new picture for us each day.

To get our attention to what He has to say.

He is a creator and has many visions for us to see and unfold.

*It is like He is leaving us messages that He
wants us to take and mold.*

*The beauty they capture is nothing like we
have ever seen here on earth.*

It is like starting fresh over again like a child at birth.

Colors that are rich and pure like our Father's heart.

It is something that none of us should have to part.

*The next time you see the paintings in the sky, look
very carefully at what they have to say.*

For who knows what He wants for us on that particular day?

*God is watching us all the time and making sure that we
stay on the path that He has chosen for each of us.*

*Do not worry, for if you follow the sunset and
sunrise, you will know that your journey is just
the beginning of His beautiful show.*

Sunsets

Sunsets are like heaven's songs

They show us there are no wrongs

They are God's beauty to share with us all.

In your heart listen for His special call.

For each color He puts into a sunset, reflects
His love for earth creatures below.

For it is something that you all should feel and know.

Life's Journey

I've walked so many miles on this land,

To look back and see all the helping hands.

There were many struggles to overcome from inside.

Sometimes I felt like and ocean tide.

To see all the accomplishments made.

There are memories that will never fade.

From being a young child sweet as can be,

To grow into a woman and see all that I've seen.

The world has many things to offer and to share.

Some things are very special and rare.

Don't ever think you've done anything wrong.

For you have a unique song.

Memories to tell to your children ahead,

*From you they will learn the meaning of
life, From all that was said.*

Heavenly Treasures

For every road there is an adventure waiting to be discovered.

When a challenge seems hard,

In the end there is always something solved.

When an image doesn't seem to be clear to your eyes,

There is a vision waititng for you to reveal that soon won't be in disguise.

When a feeling of floating on air surrounds you without warning,

Love is what may be sending your heart soaring.

When sadness or sorrow come your way,

Listen to what all life has to say.

When hatred comes along your way,

Remember compassionate words are what to say.

When you might have a failure come to pass, remember that is what makes us strong and creates character that will always last.

Courage comes from never giving in.

For determination is what makes us win.

Dreams are aspirations we have to look forward to.

Don't ever give in to people who say they can't come true.

Mistakes are when we learn to stay away from all things that are wrong.

Remember without them we would not have our own special song.

Remember it doesn't matter what size, shape, or race.

We all will be remembered for what heavenly treasures we've given to this place

Jesus, You Are My Inspiration

You are my inspiration in everything I do.

I know all Your words are blessed and true.

I think of You and a smile appears across my face.

Along with a warm feeling that cannot be replaced.

Your words flow through me like an never-ending story.

For You have touched my soul in so many ways.

Through Your teachings there is much I have learned.

That love everlasting is what is earned.

When You see things through His eyes.

You will feel the comfort of His healing
through the trying of times.

Please don't turn your back on Me.

Let Me show you everything precious there is to see.

God's Unconditional Love

Ocean tides that fall onto the land,

Pebbles that sparkle in the sand.

Skies that are blue and clouds that are soft and white,

The moon that shines on a cold winter's night.

Birds that sing their songs,

Animals that play in the fields and do no wrong.

To see the sunshine,

Children laughing and playing all the time.

To hear the wind blow,

And all of nature's glow.

To feel the strength that One holds above,

And to reach out and feel His love.

It's a feeling hard to describe,

Take time to appreciate all that He has inscribed.

Untitled

My children, remember I will never give you
anything that you cannot handle.

For sometimes you need to go through some trials
to see My eternal burning candle.

You may not know in that moment in time the answer's why.

For sometimes in order to seek and see Me
you need to have your heart cry.

I do not want you to have pain in your life My children,

but sometimes in order for you to listen and
be strong in your walk with Me.

I need you to seek within your soul and look to My signs
that I send to you to follow and want to strive to be.

For the fruits of your labor will be gratefully rewarded
in My eternal life to come, so please My children
do not ever forget where you come from.

I am with you always and will stand by your side with
this war to fight together with our armor on.

For when we are done we will be singing heaven's eternal song.

For if you remember to look for Me in these times of need and
sorrow. You will never feel like your heart was just borrowed.

For if you remember to look for Me in these
times of need and sorrow.

You will never feel like your heart was just borrowed.

*My children of God, if you remember your purpose that
I have created for only you to fill on this earth for
me; for you will truly see heaven's plan uncovered
to hold by all My messages that I have told.*

*Listen carefully each day to hear My voice
calling for you to teach My words.*

*Seek and look because they may not always be
seen by ones human eyes to see.*

But mere images of nature's voice speaking for Me.

Walk with Me

Walk with Me My child,

And feel heavens grace upon you tender and mild.

Walk in My footsteps on a journey full of peace.

Let your heart finally feel at ease.

Walk with Me and have faith in where I lead you.

I know it is not easy to follow, but know I only give you

Guidance to what is pure.

When you walk with Me at times you may feel alone.

That is when you need to hear My comforting tone.

I know at times you may stumble and fall.

That is when I will give My hand to you to help you stand tall.

I will embrace you and not let evil harm you in anyway.

I will protect you each day.

To walk with Me means certain sacrifices to make.

In the end, you will have heaven as your keepsake.

Let Me give you the courage to know that each decision is right.

You are never alone in heaven's fight.

I will take you home My child when the time is right.

Until then know I am with you every day and night.

A Beautiful Soul

A beautiful soul fills the heart.

It plays a unique song that sets the rest apart.

It lights up the world with generosity and care.

Gives without hesitation for the world to share.

Never judges for mistakes that were made.

It knows the past will always fade.

Courageous and brave to take on life's challenges that come.

To stand tall and pass each lesson taught along to someone.

*It sees beauty in everything and never takes
for granted God's blessings.*

Visions of Heaven

Skies that are blue and full of grace.

The sun that has a scintillating glow that can never be replaced.

The air as fresh as a dewdrop on an early spring morning day.

Where compassionate words are all people will say.

*A love that is passionate and deep from
anything you could ever imagine.*

What an amazing feeling to be able to express from within.

It is a miraculous place where we will never have to feel alone.

To feel the everlasting peacefulness of God's eternal home.

We can all have the chance to experience this amazing place.

That is all we have to do is have God's Amazing Grace.

Until it is our time to visit our father in heaven.

*We need to take time to appreciate all the
wonderful things He has given us.*

Single in God's Eyes

Remember My child, that being single is not a crime.

For it brings you closer to Me and all the things
I want for you to have in time.

For each lesson learned and each trail you overcome

Will bring you closer to the future that is waiting for you.

You need to look at the signs that are given to you.

And know that each one comes from Me, your
Father, who will always be true.

I will never let you fall or stray too far from Me.

For there are so many things in this lifetime I want you to see.

Sometimes you can only see them when you are alone and
hurting. That is when I will come to you and let you
know that I am there to hold you and comfort you.

I will show you that there is love waiting for
you, but only when the time is right,

And I know your heart will not have to be blue.

I cherish My time with you My child when
we get to spend it one on one.

You need to have faith in Me that I will not bring someone
in your life until I know that person deserves you
and will accept you and where you come from.

I know it is hard and not always easy to wait for the unknown.

But if you do, you will see an eternity of love that comes
from only Me, and you will no longer have to frown.

God's Blessings

My blessing's for you My child are these things…

To forgive all the people who are hurtful towards you.

To pray that their hearts heal and become pure.

To have a loving heart towards everyone in need.

To be kind to everyone you meet.

Pray that they ask for God's strength to plant their feet.

To lend a guiding hand to those who are lost.

To pray that they find their way to the cross.

To give a listening ear toward others who need comfort.

Pray that they hear God's calming voice through whatever they need help to sort.

Remember My child sometimes it takes a heart that is blessed to plant a seed.

To help those hearts that find it hard to see.

God's Guiding Hands

When I feel lost and alone, Your hand holds
onto mine to help guide me.

When I feel weak, You are my strength that
helps carry me to where I need to be.

When my vision becomes cloudy, You are
always there to help me see.

I feel Your arms around me when I am in need.

You gave me your wings to help set me free.

Life without You has no meaning.

For You are my true being.

You have touched my life in so many ways.

I thank You for each glorious day.

I have faith in everything that You do.

You are my support, foundation, security, and my friend.

I know my journey with You will be filled
with good things that are true.

I love You with all my soul.

I am so glad You're there to catch me when I sometimes fall.

God's Lessons

Have faith in Me and I will guide you.

Trust in Me and My heart is yours to hold.

Believe in Me and all good things will come your way.

Have hope that each decision I make for you will help you not to stray.

Feel My love unconditionally for you My child.

And you will know that I am with you always.

Blessings from the Heart

Blessing from the heart are treasures that can't be sold.

They are kept deep for you to feel and hold.

They are memories that last through a lifetime in your heart.

They help to remember your journey from the start.

To be thankful for each day.

To give you strength to carry you along the way.

They are what makes hearts of gold.

As you let priceless treasures unfold.

Everyday count your blessings from God's Amazing Grace.

For you will see how rich your life has been
from each heavenly trace.

My Vision of God

I had a vison one day that God was walking with me down an unknown road. He told me, "My child, this is where I want you to go, For if you have faith in Me, you will travel ahead and see what is waiting for you at the end to unfold."

I walked down the road with feelings that were overwhelming at first. Then I realized what an exciting adventure it was to see all the beauty and love that God has given to us. It made my eyes tear and my heart want to burst.

I started thinking as I was on this amazing journey that the unknown is what I must go through, while my Father is watching me and guiding me to the direction He needs me to turn to discover what is true. If you believe with all your soul and listen in the winds, you will hear the voice of your Father calling out to you.

Images came into my head of beauty that was pure and full of light. As I looked into the sun shining through the trees,

I could feel heaven's warmth holding me tight. As I walked farther down the road, I started feeling at ease and not so overwhelmed.

I knew in my heart that God would guide me and not let me stumble and fall. With each step I took, I could hear Him calling me to come and keep standing tall.

My legs were light with each step I took, like I was floating on air. All my worries were erased from my mind and I felt like there wasn't anything I couldn't bear.

When I got closer to the end of the road, I could see my Father waiting for me with His arms opened wide. I ran toward Him like an ocean tide.

He embraced me in His arms and said, My child, remember I am here to hold you, guide you, teach you, comfort and love you for all of time. Even though you do not know everything, remember that I do, and I have your future planned out for you. The only thing you have to do is listen for the call of heavenly chimes.

About the Author

Marnie Hunziker was born on March 27th in St. Louis Park Minnesota. She is in her late forties. She is single right now, which she chooses to be. She believes that Jesus will bring her soulmate to her when she is ready. Until then, she enjoys going to church, cooking, baking, writing poetry, learning the Bible and Jesus's history, going to movies and the theatre, being an Aunt to her two beautiful niece's, and spending time with family.

She had been published several times with the International Library of Poetry. She received the Editor's Choice Award for Outstanding Achievement in Poetry for "*Life's Journey*" which was published in September 2000 by the International Library of Poetry. She has been writing poetry since 1989. She would like to thank Jesus Christ for her gift of writing and being able to touch the hearts of others. Along with her mother, dad, sister and brother-in-law for all their encouragement through the years.